Collective Poems & Short Stories, Vol. 1

Collective Poems & Short Stories, Vol. 1

Sometimes
I JUST FEEL LIKE
Writing

SHEILA O'KELLEY

A Division of WINEPRESS PUBLISHING

Dedication

My grandmother, Jacquelyn Cochran,
My father-in-law, William O'Kelley Jr.,
My mother-in-law, Gladys O'Kelley.

All have gone on to be with Jesus.
Miss you guys much!

Table of Contents

Foreword

This collection of poems and short stories is refreshing. It reminds me of the poetry of David and Solomon in the Bible.

It will cause you to laugh, to cry, to nod your head, and to be amazed with the honesty of the author. This collection has certainly liberated the writer, and it will inspire you, the reader, to liberate yourself.

The truth will set you free.

God bless you, Sister Shelia!

Dr. Paulette Anderson, Evangelist
Regional Teen Convention, Founder and Coordinator
Rialto, California
www.teenconvention.org

Preface

This is a collection of poems and short stories that is focused on ministering to women, young ladies, and girls who are and were abused and hurt.

With emphasis on the African-American culture and worship services, this collection strikes a heartfelt chord in each of us for our desire to simply be loved.

I've been there, baby, and it's not all your fault. Matter of fact, most things are not your fault, but the sickness of someone else.

Now, I'm not saying you shouldn't be responsible for the things you can control. Just know that guilt can't live here anymore!

Real life...
Live it once. Live it well.
Live it right.
To Jesus' delight!

Acknowledgments

I can't say enough about the God we serve! He alone gave me a gift of taking a thought in my head and putting it into a story. Thank You, Lord, for choosing me.

Little Sheila

To my husband, William:

I love the little short guy to the mostest. You made me think and write and write and think. You laughed when I didn't think anyone would. Your laugh was the one that really mattered.

To the kids:

Jason, my firstborn: I always knew you had it in you. Needless to say, I am very pleased with the fine young man you have become.

Kevin, the middle child: Just wanna say thanks for being my Kevin.

Love, Mom

Michelle, my only girl: You are a sweetheart. I know I fuss at you, but you got it like that. (Smile!)

To my momma: Look what God did! Some stuff I told you and some I didn't, but I don't think it mattered to you. I'm still your "baby girl."

To my brothers and sister: This is a family accomplishment.

Mrs. Gladys O'Kelley (my mother-in-law): You are one fine lady! And you are a super person in God to know and love. Thanks for the true love you and Granddad showed to me.

Elder Joseph Dunn: You are like my father, and I love you much. More than an uncle, you're my Uncle Joe!

To Bishop and Dr. Montgomery: For the wisdom you have shared with me while at your assembly. Dr. Montgomery, you always told us, "No excuses, so don't look for one!"

To my good friend Cynthia: We are so different, but so much alike. Thanks for being my good friend.

Thanks to my good friend Dr. Wes Scott. In everything I have ever done, you have supported me. You are a good friend, Wes. Thank you, Elaine, for continuing to allow us to be friends.

To my family and friends in Texas, Louisiana, North Carolina, Virginia, Indiana, Washington, DC, Maryland, California, Georgia, Washington State, and many other places: Thanks!

To all of those with visual and hearing impairments: Never think of yourself as useless and incapable of achievements. The Bible says, "I can do all things through Christ which strengtheneth me" (Philippians 4:13—KJV). We are all invaluable in God's sight.

I also want to thank someone whose name I don't even know. But he once stated on a TV program, "People that are visual impaired can't do so many things, I don't even know why they try." I am so glad he said that and that I heard him.

Acknowledgments

From that day forward I knew I had to prove him wrong and myself right.

To my many well-wishers and friends…your encouraging comments and suggestions are truly appreciated.

Thanks, everybody,

Sheila

Introduction

From experiences of forty years of life, *Sometimes I Just Feel Like Writing* incorporates lifestyles and living from the West Coast to the East Coast; from the hidden beauty of the Southwest desert to the beautiful autumns of the Northeast.

This book takes a serious yet sometimes humorous look at real life, centered around experiences of being raised in the church...the church down the street, the church around the corner, the storefront, the cathedral, the oasis, the temple, the house of whatever, the big, the little, the greater, the mount... ya know, it's all the *church*!

It might not have happened to you.
Hopefully, it won't.
But it happens.

You may not have seen it.
Hopefully, you won't.
But it's there.

Some have not lived it.
Hopefully, you won't.
But some have.

Truth is truth.

~~~~~~

All of the characters in this story are fictional. Any similarities to those living or dead are coincidental.

1926...

This is my room. The rugs are from my friend Sylvia. The matching towels came from me.

I've got a mattress. When I lived at the shelter, God granted me favor there. The lady who runs it—I forgot her name—when we could stay there no longer, she gave me this bed. It's only a mattress, but it has sheets and a blanket.

The kids have the pillows on their bunk beds. Their room is right beside mine, so they're near me at all times.

I'm so proud of myself just for holding on.

I am still holding on. In the meantime, things are good... real good. Because I kept holding on to the Lord, He gave me good things.

I work full time now. Got some benefits with the job. Insurance, paid days off, and sick leave.

Soon after I got this job, I bought carpeting. Pretty color, don't you think? And that microwave in the kitchen—got that at Wal-Mart. Straight out the box. Spent $80 on it. No penny-pinching any more!

Ray from the church built me a fence. Mr. Phelps across the street gave me my ice maker. I could go on and on!

Now I just want to tell all you women who think you can't make it another day... especially you single ones... that you just have to hold on. God is gonna bless you!

The Awesomeness of My God

I am sitting on the steps of Aunt Gayle's porch. It's a sunshiny day in Georgia.

Looking up and down the street, many things come to my mind. Above all is this: My God is awesome! He took dirt and made man. Woman soon followed. And so many animals He created! From my perch on my aunt's porch, I can see squirrels, dogs, and cats, and that's just the beginning. There are countless beautiful creatures God gave to mankind

As my aunt and I go for a drive in the car, I see rivers, lakes, mountains, and many other wonderful things. From north to south, east to west, anywhere you want to look. Take a breath, feel the rays of the sun, the cool of the night. Soak in the pleasures we have.

I give glory to God. For he is my awesome God!

Just Appreciate It

This is how I see it…
    We buy, we cook, we feed you.
    'Cause we're good ol' Mom and Dad.
    You eat, get up, and leave with your friends.
    Ooh, it makes me mad!
    No "Thank you," "Love you," "Appreciate you."
    Nope, not a word.
    So, guess what I decided?
    I got a revelation.
    Took me a while, but I got it.
    When you start helping,
    buying, and feeding,
    Then you can complain, bicker, and whine.
    Till then, guys,
    Appreciate it! Be grateful!
    'Cause the day is coming when
    You're gonna miss all this.

Just thought I'd pass it along.

Babies Having Babies

Babies having babies;
Can't take care of yourself.
"I got a man," you say.
No, you got a boy.
He ain't no man!

Chest all hanging out,
Skirt up past your knees.
Fix your clothes!
You're too pretty to be looking like that.

His pants all baggy,
hangin' way down.
Don't he own a belt?

That's why you're carrying a baby.
Food stamps and "Miss Welfare."
Hey, I thought you could take care of yourself.

Go to school.
Get an education.
Stay in the church,
Under the blood.
Don't your hear the saints praying?

You think you can take care of yourself.
But, honey, you're just a baby with a baby.

Letter to My Baby Girl

Hello, baby girl! This is Momma.

Such a pretty little girl you are. Skin the color of coffee. Hair so shiny and silky.

Your Momma wants the best for you. Every doll you want, sitting on your dresser. Pretty dresses with tights and polished shoes. Even a purse of your very own.

But don't rush to grow up, baby girl. Enjoy your life. The day will come when you will like boys, talk on the phone, and start dating. Then I will miss the baby years.

One day you'll be all grown up with a daughter of your own. Like me, you will want the best for her. When you marry (if daddy lets you), I want you to be pure and holy. Let the Lord send you a man who will love you.

Until that day comes—and you've got plenty of time, you know—just enjoy being Momma's baby girl!

Love and sweet kisses,

Mom

Choir Rehearsal

The church announcement read:

Combined Choir Rehearsal
Tuesday at 7:00 p.m.
Please be on time

So I rushed to rehearsal. Man, was I beat. Didn't even get a chance to eat dinner. But that's okay. The choir was on a fast that week.

Got to the church at 6:53. But there wasn't nobody there. Not even the musicians. The head deacon was sitting in his car with the heat on. So I knew the church doors were still locked. If I said anything, he'd think I had an "attitude." So I figured I might as well keep my mouth shut.

The president of the choir finally showed up at 7:20. Looked like she ate, though, since she missed wiping off all of the mayonnaise from her mouth. Apparently the Lord didn't lead her to participate in the choir fast. Hush my mouth again.

The director drove up about 7:45. "Sorry I'm late, guys," he said. Don't know what his excuse was. I was beginning to not want to sing on Sunday.

The choir members came strolling in, all of them so late we only had time to rehearse five songs. And the pastor wonders why we sing the same songs every week.

At 9:00 the choir president got up to make some announcements. I didn't hear her say anything like "We need to work on our timeliness." If I wasn't saved, I would have knocked the hair out of her French roll. (It ain't even all her hair anyway.)

I went to the choir room to get my robe. I'm going to try to be dedicated, whether other people do right or not. Work on myself, not others. Do as unto the Lord and He will do the rest.

So, I'm still in the choir…till next rehearsal at least.

The Church Dinner

We're having a church dinner this Sunday.
Won't you join us as we eat, fellowship, and rejoice!

Mother Annie will fry the chicken, crispy through and
through.
Brother Ed…well, every year he makes something new.

Who knows who'll fix the greens or what kind they'll be.
Turnip, kale, mustard, or collard, we'll have to wait and see.

For sure there will be lots of sweet iced tea and lemonade,
These two drinks from the table will never fade.

Mashed potatoes, mac and cheese, yams, maybe rice.
Keep it simple, but make it nice!

Last of all, but not the least,
Sister Fredericks, those rolls! Made from yeast.

Well, the time has come for our dinner to end,
Thanks for coming and sharing.

Enjoy!

Dad, Dear Dad

Dad,

Why did you leave my mommy? What did she do to you? Can you tell me?

I thought you loved us, but you left us. Teacher says that's not love.

Where did you go when you left? I called your office, but the lady said you were gone. Do you have a new number?

I go to school all day now. Did you know that? I can tie my own shoes.

Mommy doesn't cry as much. Do you feel glad? She goes to my PTA meetings. I never get my name on the board.

Mommy works four days a week at the store. She goes to college too. I get to go with her sometimes when her class isn't going to have a test. I have to be real quiet, though.

Talia is my babysitter when Mom works. Do you know Talia's dad? Today for dinner we had rice and chicken. I helped. I put the chicken in the oven.

Well, Dad, I have to go. Please send me your address.

Teacher says sometimes a daddy will come back. But I think me and Mommy are okay without you.

Bye, Dad.

Johnathon
(I even know how to spell my name, Dad!)

Deliver Me, Jesus

Deliver me, Jesus, I cried,
From these burdens that I carry.
Deliver me from my husband.
You know him; his name is Barry.

Deliver me from the pain, the bruises.
It's his right arm that he always uses.

Deliver me! He says he loves me,
That he won't hurt our son Jamal…just me.

Deliver me!
I have no one to call on,
None to ask.
Didn't know I would hit the wall.

I gather up my baby.
He's only four, you know.
We deserve more than this.
Life is too short, you know.

Put the keys in the car,
Going for a ride.
Not sure where,
But I must hide.

I asked Jesus to deliver me,
And He did!
Sent me an angel.
Her name is Miss Pat.

She fed me and clothed me,
Gave us food to eat,
And told me from now on,
"Celeste, you will not be beat!"

I have a job now;
No more nightmares and bad dreams.
I asked the good Lord to do it,
And you know it seems…

He delivered me!

"Deliver me" was once my prayer.
But now, my friend, I'm almost there!

I hold my head up.
The past is behind me.
I am so glad
I asked Jesus…

To deliver me!

Dedicated to my friend Ceci, who overcame spousal abuse.
(Her name has been changed to protect her.)

Sometimes I Just Feel Like Writing

Sometimes I just feel like writing.
It's a feeling I get within.
I pick up a piece of paper,
A pencil or a pen.

It helps to clear my head
to jot down a note or two.
Hey, you never know,
Maybe this could help you.

I don't always have a clear direction,
Not sure where I'm going.
That's a really good day
To just start writing.

So much is in me,
Bottled-up hurts, pains, and fears.
Sometimes the only way to get it out
Is to just start writing.

Maybe you can understand.
I know I'm trying to go somewhere.
Where now? That is the question.

When confused, dazed, or just out of it,
I just feel like writing.

I've been through a lot,
a whole lot.
But thanks be to God,
I made it!

And when the clouds seem heavy,
The burdens too much,
Just pick up a pen.
You might just start writing!

Girls Night Out!!

It's girls night out tonight.
I'm so excited…too excited!

We'll meet at Sandra's house.
Pop the popcorn, open the chips.

Imagine grown women acting like this!
We need a break, y'all,
From life's good days and bad.
Guess who will be there?
Adria, Karla, Zsa, Robin, Vanessa,
Just to name a few.
Cynthia may even show.
She sometimes does, you know.
But no kids, husbands, or boyfriends are allowed.

What are we gonna do, you ask?
Watch a movie or two, sing a song, cry, and laugh.
When it's girls night out, you never know!

No gossip, just plain old fun.
Festivities start at 7 p.m. sharp.
Be there or be square!
Come join us and let your hair down.

Grandma Died Today

The phone rang while I was asleep. I opened my eyes to see the clock. 5:00.

"Hello," I whispered.

"Sheila, this is Mom. I called to tell you that your grandma died today."

"No!" I cried out. Not my grandma!

Every ounce of grief and pain that was within me came out in long sobs of sorrow. I lay back in the bed. I heard my husband talking to my mother, trying to console her for losing her mother. All I knew was that my grandma had died that day. I cried, moaned, and sobbed.

After my husband hung up, he gathered me in his arms. "Shhh, it's okay." He softly stroked my hair.

When I finally stopped crying I thought, *Dear God, what are we gonna do without my grammie around?*

Jason came upstairs to our room with tears in his long eyelashes. He uttered not a word.

William told us both that God had granted Grandma peace by taking her out of her sickness, out of intensive care, and into His arms.

I listened to him but didn't really hear him. He was saying real nice things. But at that moment, all I knew was that my grandma was gone.

Around six o'clock, I went downstairs. Had to start washing the dishes, cleaning the clothes, sweeping the floor. I was really just occupying time and space. I needed to think, though I didn't even know what I needed to think about.

I phoned my friend Bernard. I had to tell someone.

"Hey, Sis," he said. "What's up?" He sounded tired.

"My grandma died today."

Before he could respond, I started shaking. I dropped the phone on the bed. My head was pounding.

My husband picked up the receiver, said a few words to Bernard, then hung up.

I crawled under the covers and thought, *This is going to be a long day.*

Grandma was the backbone of our family. The solid rock. When my dad walked out on us, Grandma was there. When I had my children, she was there. Lost a job and got a new one, she was there. Failed marriage, successful marriage, every trial and triumph of my life, she was there.

The lessons she taught me can't all be printed. Some of them I dare not share. Maybe I'll tell my children, for they are her future generation.

When I was eleven she tried to teach me how to make biscuits. I wasn't interested in cooking, but that day I sure acted like it. My hands went in the flour with her wrinkled hands. Hands that showed what life on the assembly line will get you. She'd labored in the cannery plant for long, hard days and sometimes nights.

When my brother needed a button sewn on his shirt, he pulled up a chair beside her and got his lesson in mending.

My daughter received her first cooking lesson at age ten. She peeled, cut, and mashed the potatoes, then cooked them with just the right amount of butter. That's the kind of lesson you can't get out of a cookbook.

When I married my husband in 1990, Grandma told me, "Baby girl, just be happy."

She has now been laid to rest. The service has come and gone. She looked beautiful that day in her white suit and ringlet curls around her face. I think of her often.

Lord, I know You took Grandma for a good reason. And I know she has no more sickness or pains in her body. But I still have to live with the fact that my grandma died.

Dedicated to my grandma,
Jacquelyn Cochran
• Sunrise, April 4, 1926-July 9, 2000, Sunset •

He Had the Nerve

This man of mine!
I married him a few years ago.
Things were pretty good for a while.
But then one day he went plum fool crazy.
He got urges…of the wrong sort!

He had the nerve to go and get some grub,
Even though we had food right there at home.
He left me, sitting there, saying, "I'll be back."
Instead he left me all alone.

Then he had the nerve to say to me,
"It's for the church."
Guess that's supposed to make me feel better.
But I'm the one who's been left behind!

Then he had the nerve to minister to the youth,
To help other people's kids.
His own kids were borderline,
Back stabbers and crazy!

Before he got the next nerve,
I got up the nerve to tell him,
"Before you can help people with their kids,
You've got to get your own house in order.
And then you can go…
Please go…
With my blessings."

Hidden Hurts

I've got some hidden hurts
Locked way back in the corner of my mind.
At least that's where I think I put 'em.

There is a failed relationship, and a stale one,
And the one I'm in now.
Oh, I'm happily married,
But I've still got hidden hurts.

I was a teen mom.
I made up a man's name to put on the birth certificate.
My child had an "invisible father."

My momma wasn't crying tears of joy when the doctor told her
    she had a grandchild.
She raised Scooter for me.
And I never got around to telling him he was my son and not
    my brother.

I once lived on "heroin row."
T-ball was my pimp from '88 to '90.
Some days I didn't even get paid.

The preacher man says the church is my refuge.
It's supposed to be the healing place for the wounded.

But the people at church hurt me too.
They bring up my past all the time.
I've been told I'm not fit to sing with the Gospel Chorale.
I can't sit up front cause those pews are reserved for "praisers only."

When will I have my "Praise Break"?

One woman told me to go to a class.
It was called "Woman, Thou Are Loosed."
"For what?" I asked her.
"I'm not loosed; I've got hurts."

Then one day, I met a lady.
She came to the back, where all the castaways sit.
She grabbed my hand, picked up a box of tissues, and took me to the pastor's office.

There he broke me down,
Told me to release those hidden hurts
And allow God to wipe my slate clean.

"Live no more on Misery Circle," he said.
If I live right, he promised, heaven belongs to me.

So I let them all go,
Right there in the office.

I got on the floor.
I moaned, groaned, screamed, and kicked.
Then I got up.

Two years later now, I am free.
I am married to Julian.
Scooter, my son, will graduate from high school in four months.

I have moved on.
Moved up.
No more hidden hurts.
Just delicious days of enjoying life!

I Got To

I got to cook,
Even when I don't want to.

I got to listen to you,
Even when I don't want to.

I got to give you some,
When I definitely don't want to.

Talk the talk.
Walk the walk.

I got to stand beside you,
Even when I don't want to.

Clean, wash, sweep,
When I don't want to.

Guess what?

I'm going with the girls tonight.
"Why?" you ask.

Because I want to!

He's Locked Up

I'm waiting for the bus.
It comes around 9:10 or 9:15.
Going to see my brother.
Last summer, you see, he got locked up.

Can't blame anyone.
No wrong place, wrong time.
He did it all himself.
Legal fees cost more than a few dimes.
Had to spend a lot just for getting locked up.

Tony won't be home for Easter, Christmas,
Thanksgiving, or anything in between.
Mom feels bad.
My sister is sad.
And me...well, he's my brother.
And he got locked up.

Last month I sent him some money.

He said he needed some stamps.
He made a bad mistake.
But I felt like I had to help him.

The bus is here now.
I'll have to take a seat.
I won't get to hug him or touch him.
Might have to cry through the glass.
But this is how life is
When your brother gets locked up.

Mad, Just Mad

Why did he get mad?
What made him mad this time?
Why is he mad at me?

What did I say?
What did I do?
Nothing is ever right.
He's very hard to please.

Mad about this.
Mad about that.
Mad, mad, mad, just mad.
I'm sick of mad.

If I'd known he was mad,
I would have never come home.
Boy, this is really bad.

Did he not like dinner?
Was the TV too loud?
Bad day at work?
Does it have something to do with me?
Or is he just mad.

Mad today.
Mad tomorrow.
Mad next year.
What a wonderful life.

Husband is mad
Wife is mad.
Kids are mad.
Even the dog is mad.

I live with a bunch of mad people.
I look for the day
When all is not mad.
But for now, he's just mad.

On This Day

I wasn't having a good day.
So I said, "I'll throw a party."
Picked up the phone right then and there.
Called Ms. Pity and invited her over.

Made me a list
Of not-so-good things
Going on today.

My brother and my sister
Are still in their "situations."
That's not a good thing.

The dog, the cat, and the fish are sick.
That's not too good, either.

Broke, no food, hair raggedy.
Nope, not good.

Husband whining, body hurting.
Lots of not-good things.

Then I opened the paper.
Today's paper.
Didn't see my name in the obituary column.
Now, that's a good thing!

Opened the blinds and let the sun shine in.
Wow! A really good thing!

Told Ms. Pity she was excused,
The party was over.
That was a great thing!

Got out of bed, pulled myself together.
I started to feel some good things.
Got in my car, drove past the shelter
Then I thought, *This is a good thing!*

In that block of time,
When I thought I'd have a not-so-good day,
I woke up to reality.

Bad things will always come my way.
But I can be grateful, ever so grateful.
Because those not-so-good things
Give me great days!

Party of Five

I'm Tanzie, and this is my story about my Party of Five. I'm just givin' you a peek. Don't tell nobody. It's nobody's business, you know. Just me and my Jesus. Oh, yeah…and you!

The date is set. Next Friday at 6 p.m. My apartment. It's small, but I only live here with me and myself.

I don't need a condo. Ain't got that kind of money anyway. You coming or not? If not, fine, I don't care.

Grandma says I need an "attitude adjustment." But I just don't have time for people and their games.

Now, back to the party…

I invited the Tyler twins: Disappointment and Discouragement. They were born three minutes apart, and they look identical.

Pity is coming (she's here all the time anyway). Hope-for-Tomorrow and Praise-in-Spite-Of completes my list.

Everyone needs to RSVP by Monday. That's just two days away. The Tyler twins (Discourage and Disappoint) handed me a note while they were walking around church taking the offering. A tacky way to respond, if you ask me! They probably had to latch onto someone else and were pressed for time.

I saw Pity this morning before I left for the early service. I don't know how that child ends up at my window all the time. Chelaine says if I let her in she will stay there forever and a day. She could be right.

Now, Hope is just way too happy for me. She left me a cheerful message on the phone.

"Tanzie, this is Hope-for-Tomorrow." She talks like she is singing a song. "Of course, I will be at your party!"

She even gave me a Scripture. "Remember," she said, "you can do all things through Christ who strengthens you. See ya Friday!"

I sometimes wonder why she's always so happy and hopeful. Does she ever go through any trials? Does she have dark, cloudy days? Or is the sun ever present for her?

I know Hope-for-Tomorrow has had some rough days. She's a single mother of three, works two jobs, and she doesn't receive any child support from her deadbeat ex-husband.

How can she be such a bright light in a dark world?

Even though we go to the same church, I don't have what she has. Maybe I need to move to her side of town. Sit a little closer to her in church.

If I remember correctly, Hope graduated three years ahead of me.

But my diploma should say something like this:

Tanzie Franks
"School of Hard Knocks"
Class of 1999
She graduated top of her class!

Hold on a second. Someone is at the door.

Oh, great! It's Pitiful Woman. (We call her Pity for short.) She came to remind me that I have less than eight dollars in the bank, that two checks bounced, and that KT left me for another woman (a woman who used to be my friend).

And did I tell you my company is downsizing? I may not even have a job in about three months. Already my fridge is riding on empty.

"You might want to re-think this party thing," Pity tells me. I thank her for her "tip of the day" but tell her I'm going to do it anyway. I'm not feeding an army, just five folks.

Mom says I need to get under Pity's shadow and kick her out. But Pity has been there when other folks couldn't be found. She's not leaving my life that easy.

Discouragement Tyler told me she could come over early and help me set up.

The Tyler twins are well known at the church. They've been on the floor near the altar after many a woman has fallen out to Jesus.

Disappointment will be there, too, but later on. Surprisingly, I don't feel disappointed!

Of course Praise is coming. Now, that girl has a story to tell. Somebody needs to call Oprah and let her tell the "real story."

The In-Spite-Of family has been through hell and back three or four times.

Praise's momma died from sugar diabetes, and her daddy just lost every bit of sense he used to have. I guess the sense he did have left when they started putting dirt on her momma's coffin at the cemetery. I think he had to stay at a mental health hospital for a few years after that.

Praise's daughter, Glorious, went home to be with Jesus at the age of three months. Some kind of rare birth defect, and her body never quite matured.

But Praise can be found in the front row at every church service. Even when the pastor and his wife ain't there, she is.

She comes when the regulars are too tired. I invited her to my party 'cause she has a knack for fighting the devil and pressing on.

I'm trying to get where she and Hope are in Christ. Pity told me she really didn't want Praise there, but Pity will be Pity no matter who comes.

It's party day!

Discouragement did show up early. Real early. She told me my veggie tray looked a little skimpy. But I didn't see anything in her hand when she came to the door!

I opened the mini-blinds, but she closed them. "Don't want too much sunshine in your life," she said.

I yanked them back open. This is my place, after all!

Disappointment called at the last minute and said she won't be able to bring the punch after all. Great! Now we won't have anything to drink.

Just a sec. The phone is ringing.

"Tanzie, this is Hope-for-Tomorrow," she says with that everlasting ring in her voice. "Skylar's has fruit punch on sale. I have an extra buck or two. Should I pick some up?"

"Please!" I say.

"I had some chips at home," she adds. "So I'm bringing those too."

Things are starting to look brighter. Maybe there is hope after all.

I wonder if Hope realizes how much her phone call meant to me.

Discouragement lets me know she counted only five napkins while I was on the phone with Hope. I go to the kitchen and grab some paper towels.

I can't believe my phone is ringing again. It's Pity.

"My tire is flat. I won't be able to get spoons." I only have three.

Disappointment calls her sister, Discouragement, on the cell. She says they need to go over to the Maxies' house. It seems the Maxies just had a house fire and lost everything, and the twin's mom, Bitter Tyler, told them to get over there right away.

I am not sorry to see her go.

Hope calls to say she's running late. Her son, Justin Time, is still at baseball practice at Timberlake Park. She will be here, though.

For right now, it's just me and Pity. She points out my mismatched furniture and broken chairs, and tells me all about the singles conference last week that I wasn't able to go to.

"Thanks," I mumble.

"You know Pastor Mark is always saying, "Your blessing is on the way!"

He said that six months ago. I've been trying to forget that sermon. His message was for others, and they already got their blessings. I'm still sitting here waiting on mine.

"Not all messages are for everybody," Pity says. "Sometimes you'd do better not to look for anything, 'cause nothing's coming your way anyhow."

The doorbell rings. It's Praise!

Pity rolls her eyes. "Who invited her?" Pity whines.

"I did," I shoot back at her.

I need Praise-in-Spite-Of every now and then.

Pity sits on the couch with her legs crossed. She reminds Praise that her sister, Shall-be-Saved, is still using crack cocaine, her tithe check bounced, and she didn't get the Section-8 house she put in.

"Well," Praise tells Pity, "you're right about everything. But I just have this deep-down praise in me that won't stop." She's almost preaching!

I just sit there. This is what I need to hear. Straight to the point, food for my soul.

Praise tells Pity that she serves a God who is more than able to do exceedingly abundantly above all that she can ask or think.

So, Pity, take *that* to your *own* party!

Still, I only have three spoons. And where is Hope-for-Tomorrow? She said she would be here.

Pity tells me to choose between her and Praise. "You can't have us both here. It won't work. We don't sit well with each other."

I start to shake and cry.

Pity reminds me of what I have lost.

Praise tells me where I can find those things again. She reminds me of the chains that can be broken and stay broken.

After a few more tears, a hug, and a high-five, I put a smile on my face. When I look up, Pity has left through the same window she came in through.

Hope is here!

"Discouragement and Disappointment had to leave early," I tell her. "Pity got fed up and went looking for some other window to climb in."

So now it's just me and Hope-for-Tomorrow and Praise-in-Spite-Of. And I have exactly three spoons for the melted ice cream!

I roll on the floor with Hope and do a little foot-stomping with Praise.

We put on gospel and praise CDs and have a Praise Party in my house.

What the devil meant for my destruction, God turned around and used for His construction.

The Bible says, "Let the redeemed of the Lord say so,…"[2] Well, I am saying so!

The devil thought he had me, but I got away. I stand in victory!

The hidden hurts have left too.

Every time I see Pity creeping in the window, I start singing a song of praise. Filling the room with an atmosphere of worship. I praise Jehovah-Jireh and the King of Glory.

Who is the King of glory? The Lord God mighty in the battle.[3]

If you're looking for a sad song, go elsewhere. I am not defeated!

Late in the midnight hour God turned it around for me. He is my Hope-for-Tomorrow and I have a Praise-in-Spite-Of.

When you come to church, look for me in the front row with the Praisers!

You can praise Him too. The more you praise Him, the more He'll bless ya!

Thanks to Discouragement, Disappointment, and Pity, I now walk in the fullness of knowing God. He did it for me. He will do it for you too!

Tanzie Franks

Real Life

The food stamps came, but they're gone.
The welfare check is spent.
Food bank said I can't come in till the seventeenth.

I need a job. Ain't got no loot.
My girl left me.
She said, "You're sorry! You're tired!
"I can do better without you."

Right now, I know she's right.

I'm twenty-five years old.
But I got a vision. I saw the light.
I'm gonna be somebody.

I went to college and saw the worker.
Got me a grant. Got a job.
And now, I'm working!

Got my own place.
Got some loot and a ride.
Got my girl back and my pride.

See ya, man, at the bank.
That's where I'll be.

Then was then, and this is now.
Life is great!

A Sista's Hair

Okay, sisters, I know what it's like.
Make that appointment.
Get the relaxer.
Straighten them naps!
It's only $60.

Oh, you wanna do braids?
Where's your $150?
Have money, will braid.
Oh, you brought cash!
You gonna be here for seven hours.

Want a hot press?
For you, Grandma,
The pressing comb stuff is ancient.

Madame C. J. Walker.
Dead and gone and still making money
Lying flat in that grave.

Afro? Oh, no!
We're going way back now.
Angela Brown,
She's still making money off them pictures.

Yeah, we do Afros.
Not many, but hey,
What the customer wants, they get!

Ultra Sheen,
Our people know the name.
It will work on your hair.

Your son wants a what?
Oh, a fade, you say.
We do that too.

J. T. the barber?
That bro can put a zig-zag in your hair.

You only spent four hours at the shop?
Girl, you're doing good!

That's the life of
Sista girl and her hair!

Song of Solomon

This is my story
This is my song
Praising my Savior
All the day long
This is my story
This is my song.[1]

The title of this chapter might make you think that this is about the book from the Old Testament in the Bible. But it's not. That's a love story, and there's not much love on these pages.

My name is Nicole Lachelle Solomon. I've had a long, tough journey and I thought I'd share some of it with you. I'm hoping that if I tell you what happened to me, it won't be repeated by you or another sister.

My husband, Tyrone, was an elder at our old church. When he fell from grace, my world came sliding down right beside him.

I hadn't done anything wrong. But the walls came tumbling down on me all the same. And just like Humpty Dumpty, nobody could put me back together again.

In the Beginning

One thing I'll say about Tyrone is that the man could preach. And he didn't need the organ or drums to back him up. Didn't even need an "Amen!" or a "Hallelujah!" He was plenty powerful on his own.

He didn't use notes; he preached from the Bible to the mike. Hellfire and brimstone always fell down about five minutes into his message.

One summer, Tyrone was preaching to a standing-room-only congregation and even the host pastor got a touch of the Holy Ghost. For a minute, I thought the man was going to dance out of his clothes!

But somewhere along the way, something started to go wrong.

I guess I should have seen the warning signs. But when your husband is a preacher, you don't think you need to look over your shoulder.

One Friday he left to preach for an out-of-state church dedication. He wasn't going to be returning until Saturday, so I took our son, Jauntee, to a football game.

Tyrone's plane flew into the regional airport at 7:45 p.m. Since we only live about twelve minutes from there, I expected him home around eight.

When he came walking into the bedroom at three a.m., it was obvious he hadn't come straight home. And I didn't think he spent all that time thanking God for safe travel.

He didn't offer an explanation. So I didn't ask for one. After all, Tyrone and I loved each other. He was a pastor, and I could trust him. Besides, I was the obedient and submissive wife I knew God wanted me to be.

But I know dirt when I see it and smell it.

We lived a very comfortable life. Our three-bedroom house was almost paid for. Ty was well up the executive ladder at MediaSearch.com and I had my own part-time interior design business.

We spoiled Jauntee rotten. As the only child, I figured he should have everything, and Tyrone made sure he got it.

Things were good. Until…

Let There Be Light

I knew I'd paid the credit card bill last month. So I was shocked when they called to tell me we were over our limit by $80.

"No big deal. Just a courtesy call," the rep said.

I disputed the charges and waited for the new bill.

When it came in the mail, I noticed charges for a very expensive restaurant (that I'd never been to), some lingerie (that I didn't own), and a cell phone (that I wasn't talking on).

I decided to confront Tyrone about it that very night. But he was at a ministry meeting, and those always ended late. By the time he got home, I had a terrible headache. I decided to wait.

The next day he got a request to preach the following Sunday at a church out of town. I threw the letter under the bed.

Lord, forgive me, I prayed. *But right now, he don't need to be preaching to anybody!*

I tried to put my finger on the root of the problem. Was it money, a woman, both? And why? Was not I enough for him? Our intimate times were good. I was satisfied at least. So why would he look for something more elsewhere?

I'd always though we were close. But now I began to wonder if it was just a game.

I felt confident that I was attractive. I even still had my pre-pregnancy figure.

Tyrone was only the second man I ever dated. The first died in a car crash. After that, I was reluctant to do the dating thing again. But I gave Tyrone a chance.

And now it looks like he blew it. Guess you don't get too many chances in the world of life. He couldn't deny the things he had done (nor did he try to). I never heard the words "I'm sorry."

We do keep in touch because of our son and that's about it.

Women of God just do me one favor, please. Be prayerful and careful when it comes to men and 'yes', a man of God falls in that circle also.

Nicole Solomon (with my head held up not down)

Strange Spirit

I am not an overly zealous Christian. But I do believe in God and His power to work in our lives.

My friend Raylene invited me to a revival in Torette. The head speaker was a man named Sounder Phillips.

He was a "traveling evangelist," which meant either that he didn't stay in one place for long or that he was a pastor who went outside his own church to preach to other people.

Raylene explained that his hometown of Torette had a population of about 355 people, so most of his preaching was done in neighboring cities.

I decided to go out of curiosity. I wanted to see what a person with a name like Sounder looked like.

So, on Friday night, Raylene and I went to see this preacher named Sounder Phillips.

Boy, could he preach!

But the change that came over folks after his sermon was…well, strange.

Torette's Secrets

Torette is a weird town. Last time I was in town, we buried my uncle Gus. That was at least ten years ago.

At Vick's Diner, shrimp, crawdads, and fried okra are always in ample supply. Dot and Mae are the two waitresses who work the eighteen tables. They've been doing it so long they know plenty of secrets. But they won't tell you anything except stuff about the menu. They need to keep their jobs.

Mae is about forty-five, and she knows that Vick has a back room behind the diner. It's a small room that holds maybe twelve people comfortably. The door is always dead bolted, and only Vick and his cousin Harp have keys to it.

Every Saturday night, about 11:15, a bunch of religious nuts start showing up, and Vick takes them into that back room. The diner closes at nine, so no customers are still hanging around that late.

Mae has stayed to watch them a few times. Why those people have to lie on the floor on top of their Bibles is beyond her! She never sees Sounder lying out on the floor like that.

Mae remembers Sounder coming into the diner as a toddler. He would sit and play while his momma, Jean, would lie on the floor calling, "Jesus!" Mae always wondered if that crazy stuff would get into the little boy.

When Sounder got older, his momma took him to Saturday night prayer meetings. In his teens he started carrying around a big King James Bible that his granddad had left for him when he passed. He read it all the time.

Mae heard around town that the boy could quote Scriptures left and right. She wasn't at all surprised to hear he had been "called to the ministry" in his early twenties.

Sounder did a trial sermon at High Tower Baptist. It was a quiet church. No tambourines, drums, or other "noisemakers" allowed there. But when Sounder spoke, many people felt the power of God moving. They started raising their arms and shouting praises to the Almighty.

Even Phil Cummings, owner of the local paper, had tears in his eyes. That man had the heart of a brick.

When the local hotel owner, who used to provide girls for the hotel patrons, went to the altar, Raylean and I knew the changes were some strange ones. One minute he was a devil in disguise and the next a walking minister in the making. The man's momma prayed until the day she died for his salvation and yet Sounder does one sermon and bam! A change has come. Good, but Sounder's ways were still strange.

What had happened to these people? Buck Sanford said he thought Sounder had put poison on their programs. But God was simply showing His power to break the unbreakable.

That was what Sounder was commissioned to do; bring in the "unbringables." The good Lord had told him so Himself!

"Think it not strange," the Lord said to him in a whisper. "You will bring in those who are at hell's door."

Some folks didn't understand him. But that's okay. There are plenty of things Sounder doesn't understand himself! But he has the gift of bringing people back from the brink.

Reverend Jeremiah came to him one day while he was eating at Vick's. "Son," he said, "I want you to take the gospel of Christ on the road."

Sounder was shocked.

"What road?" he asked. Torette only had a few roads.

"I am sending you to the highway and hedges," the reverend went on.

"What if they won't hear me?" Sounder asked.

"They will hear God through you," the reverend assured him.

The reverend sent him to Mailee, Louisiana, with money for food and lodging.

Sounder thought it strange that a twenty-three-year-old would be sent out to the wolves. And what the Lord was going to do was even stranger. Yet he reminded himself that the work of the Lord is not strange. It is good and it is all good.

On a Mission to Mailee

Sounder arrived in Mailee on a Tuesday. The revival was scheduled for Wednesday and Thursday nights.

When he checked into the hotel, flies and mosquitoes flew into the room with him. The air was so thick with moisture, his Bible was picking up his sweat and he was afraid the pages would melt.

Pastor Keller and his wife welcomed Sounder with open arms. "We've heard great things from Jeremiah about you, Son," he said.

"Thank you, sir," Sounder said.

They told him church would start at seven p.m., so they would pick him up at 6:30. He could use the church office to prepare himself.

Sounder was about as nervous as a man getting married. His stomach churned, but he dared not eat anything lest it might come back up.

When they arrived at the church, the saints were already praying. The temperature outside was 86 degrees, and it felt like 99 inside.

Church fans were waving about ninety miles an hour. Ceiling fans were humming, but no air was coming from them.

Everything started off smoothly. The choir sang a long rendition of "Blessed Assurance." Although how those folks managed to sing in robes in that heat, only God knows.

As Sounder got up to preach the Word, sweat fell like water from his forehead.

He took his time and laid out the foundation. There were a few amens here and there. Natural for this neck of the woods.

When he ended the sermon, he called for a prayer line, not really sure if anyone would come.

When Skeet Monroe stood and came to the altar, Pastor Keller almost had a stoke. He had been preaching to "Bootlegger Monroe" (the locals' nickname) for eighteen years. Ol' Skeet had only come to church on Easter and Christmas. It was shocking enough that he came out that night, but that he went up to repent of sins? Strange!

But the tears forming in Skeet's eyes were real all right.

On the second night of the two-day revival, four people gave their lives to the Lord. Folks who hadn't mentioned the name of the Lord in a year became deacons and ushers.

What was it about Sounder?

He wasn't that strange after all. The folks in Torette needed a change. The change was good and God had shown himself strong once again.

He calls who He wants to call, when He wants and how He wants.

The Independence of Movette Bailey

I need to go to the store. Lucile's Fast Mart will do just fine. Can't get there, though. Don't have nobody to take me.

Harlan is still at work. I'm kind of on his time. He don't leave the plant till his second shift is over. I just need a couple of things. Eggs, a pint of milk, and maybe enough apples to make some sauce or cider.

My sister Joann always told me I need to learn how to get out on my own. "Movette," she would say, "you need to learn how to do for yourself."

People always tell you what to do and how to do it, but they ain't there when you need 'em.

I want to be independent. But Harlan's been taking me to the market for the past fifteen years or so. Never needed a car, much less a license.

Then something got a hold of me…

It was women's Sunday at church. There must have been forty or fifty of us dressed in our pretty whites.

Sister Cook said a guest speaker was coming to the 3:00 service. Her name was Ms. Myrtle Brook-Miree.

She wore a fancy suit. Rose colored, with shoes and purse to match. She told us her story…

Myrtle had a good husband who took care of her. All she had to do was keep the house, the kids, and the dog. Give him some lovin' every now and then. In exchange she could live in heaven on earth.

Then she got a phone call. Mr. Miree had a heart attack and died. In the twinkling of an eye. Here one minute and on to glory the next.

Following the burial, the church folk looked after her for a while. But there came a time when she was all on her own.

After a few amens and some hand-clapping, Myrtle told us how to have our own "Independence Day."

That Sunday Ms. Myrtle gave bus tokens to all the women at the meeting. I never thought I would be able to ride a bus. Didn't even know that the #18 bus stop was right around my corner. But Myrtle said that if I caught the bus there, all I had to do was walk about four minutes farther to get to Tompkins Day-Old Breadbox. And it would only cost 75 cents, plus a dime for the transfer.

I nervously took three tokens.

"Good for you, Movette," exclaimed Shirley Lester, loud enough for all the women to hear. "I know you not getting out the house!"

Mother Emma, the pastor's wife, gave me a half smile. I know she don't go anywhere either. But I saw her take one token.

The next day, I caught the Bunter Heights bus. Went to Walgreen's and paid the phone bill in person.

This could be all right, I thought. *Maybe I can do for myself. I can do more than cook, clean, and keep Harlan happy.*

After I learned to catch the bus, I started writing checks, and even balancing the bank book. That way, I knew that when Harlan was gone, I could do for myself.

The women's group announced an outing to a factory outlet. I sure wanted to go. But nobody could take me and I'd never been to a single outing in all my years of going to the church.

Go ahead and smile, 'cause you already know! I didn't catch the bus, though; I took a taxi. Paid my fare and bought $18 worth of junk. I loved it!

I'm so glad Ms. Brook-Miree came to speak at our church that day. No more sitting and waiting on other folk for me!

Next week, I plan to go to the community college and learn how to use this thing called a computer.

Look at me. I've been redeemed to the life of an independent woman!

Movette Bailey

The Usher, the Note, and Me

It's Sunday morning at New Hope Church. It happens to be "First Sunday." For some reason, everybody and their momma comes to church on First Sunday. Matter of fact, this is the only Sunday some of these folks come!

I decided to sit up close this Sunday. 'Bout the fourth row back or so.

But this big-boned woman sat right in front of me. And she was wearing a big ol' hat. That monster-size thing must have weighed twelve pounds at least. I couldn't see a thing!

So I jotted down a note to the usher. It said, "Please ask that lady to take off her hat so I can see. Sister Mary."

When I gave the note to the usher and she read it, she leaned down close to my ear and whispered, "I can't tell her that!"

"Why not?" I asked.

"Do you see how big that lady is?"

Then Ms. Usher went and sat down.

With a sigh I looked forward and realized I had missed the choir processional. Then the big lady grabbed a fan out of her purse and started waving it, right in front of my face!

I fussed and fumed and squirmed in my seat all through the service. Around 12:30, when the service was almost over, the big lady finally took off her hat. I couldn't believe it!

I wondered what had made her do that now. Later, I found out that other people in the church had passed so many notes to the usher that she actually got up the nerve to ask her to take off her hat.

So, if you are a big lady, when you go to church, please, please…

DON'T WEAR A HAT!

The Walls Talked

I went to church yesterday and guess who I spoke with?

Nope, it wasn't the bishop or the pastor's wife. I actually sat down and talked to the walls! And boy, did they have a story to tell.

Actually, a few stories…

The walls said, "Those kids come out of the fellowship hall and run down the steps at a mighty fast pace! Where are those kids' mothers?"

Well, that girl's momma is in the tarry room, trying to help someone get the Holy Ghost. Her kids are running through the church while she's up there. She should be minding her family. Family first, tarry later, I say.

"You didn't go to the Sunday school teacher's meeting, did ya?" another wall said.

"That superintendent got on all of the teachers for being late and unprepared. Boy, did he let 'em have it!

The finance wall said, "Oh, puh-lease. Y'all ain't heard nothing. Deacon Lighten and Deacon Grimes ain't in here counting money for no forty-five minutes. They be talking and gossiping. Used to be a sin, you know. And I think Grimes be calling in his lotto numbers."

"Hey," he said, "What the pastor don't know won't hurt him!"

The last wall to speak was the wall leading out of the sanctuary. "Brother Timmons was talking to Sister Slade (who's married)," that wall said, "and they weren't talking about the next fellowship meeting!"

"I also saw another sister rolling her eyes all up and down the back of the old lady usher. But the folks here love each other, you know. They might not like each other, but they love each other!"

The walls see, hear, and observe. And sometimes they take notes. So watch what you do within the walls of this church, 'cause they just might tell!

To My Sister

Have you ever wanted to walk out,
But you had nowhere to go?
Wanted to cry, but no tears would come?

Have you ever picked up the phone,
But nobody was home.

"Get with the program!" people say.
"Better recognize, honey, that
Every day ain't full of sunshine.
Gotta make your own self happy."

Have I ever?
Yes, I have.
Will I ever?
Maybe I will, maybe I won't.

All I know is, I might.

Trumpet Man

Ray's Place. Now, that was the joint! A storefront coffee shop for book lovers.

On Saturday afternoons they had what they called "Open Mic Night."

"Bring your talent with you." the sign read.

One day this guy got up there. He kinda fumbled a bit, then took something out of the case he had. I thought it was a sax, but it turned out to be a shiny trumpet. He polished it off as he spoke to the audience.

"My name is Max," he said. Sounded a little nervous.

With all eyes glued to him, he began to blow. And did he blow! Hit notes the coffee shop hadn't heard in years!

Played from his heart.

Chords came out of that trumpet so clear you just knew Max had a story to tell.

After playing a while, Max sat down and took a break. After a round of applause, he started talking. Said he was from Oklahoma City.

Long ways from home, I thought. *How did he get all the way here to Texas?*

Before he got up to play, I had noticed him with a guy named Kevin. Everybody at Ray's Place knew Kevin.

"Got into some troubles in Oklahoma," Max said. "Had to move on. So one day I hopped on a Greyhound bus—didn't even know where it was going—and bam! I'm on my way to Abilene, Texas. Didn't know nobody here, and didn't want to know nobody."

When he first arrived in Abilene, he said, he stayed at the YMCA. Only cost him $11 a week.

One day, as he was walking down Montana Avenue, he saw Ray's Place. Saw the blue lights in the back that said Deli.

Happened to be a Saturday, "Open Mic Night." He asked Stanley, the man in charge of the show, if he could play the following week.

Stanley shrugged and said, "Sure. Be here at 2:00. For $3.00 you can play three songs."

Max figured, *What have I got to lose?*

So he went back to the Y, took out his trumpet, and polished it. Made it look just like new. Then kissed it and put it back in the case.

That Saturday he showed up at Ray's at 2:00 sharp. He was number seven, last on the list.

When his turn came, he took the trumpet out of case and polished it again. When he began to blow, the notes came out like sweet water. Smooth sounds flowed though Ray's Place that day.

The Trumpet Man made his mark!

Every tune he played told a story. The audience was mesmerized. The hopes and dreams of life were played out in note after note.

I will never forget Ray's Place, the deli, and Max the Trumpet Man.

Walking Away

Purgatory—That place that's supposed to be between heaven and hell—well, I used to live there.

I was between a rock and a hard place. And my only friend was Ms. Lonely.

I had left my husband of eight years (Jerome), my son (Christian), my house, my dog (Spike), and my Momma, Ms. Anne Sanders. But the only person who knew I was planning to leave was my dear friend Nicelle.

She said she understood. She may not have agreed, but she tried to see where I was coming from. She told me to be strong because a lot of people weren't gonna be very happy with me.

You know, it's easier for a woman to leave her abusive husband if just one person can agree with her on what she is doing.

I decided to meet Jerome for lunch one day and try to explain it to him. We met at Slinky's Hot Dog & Pretzel Stand because it was close to Jerome's office. He had no idea of the bomb I was about to drop in his lap.

The CEO of JDS, a computer chip firm, Jerome was a gorgeous black man: six-foot-two, medium build, 210 pounds. Yet I was walking away.

I sat in the corner booth and contemplated my words. Trying to make sure my voice sounded confident.

When he walked up to the booth, he kissed me lightly on the lips.

Oh, Lord, I thought, *don't make this any harder for me.*

"What's up with my Nellie-Bear?" he said. He never did call me by my full name, Janelle. "Do you need more money? Want to paint the house? Oh, I know! You want a new car. You got it, Babe. Anything you want."

This is part of the problem.

"Jerome," I said, "I need you to know that I love you ever so much."

"Uh-oh," he replied.

"I need to go away for a little while," I blurted out. "I need to be by myself. And I don't know when...or if...I'm coming back."

Silence joined us at the table as I waited for a response.

Finally Jerome laughed out loud. "You leaving me? Who for?"

"There is no one, Jerome." I spoke quietly.

"What you gonna do when you get wherever you goin'? Work?"

I hadn't worked a day in my life. I didn't have any skills.

"I don't know. But I need to go away and find myself. Find the *real* Janelle. I'm tired of doing for everyone else and never filling my dream cup."

"So go on a vacation," he grumbled, "by yourself if you want!"

"That's not enough," I said.

"And when you do find yourself, then what will you do?"

"I don't know," I said again. Agitation sat where silence once was.

The waitress stopped by our booth offering coffee. I waved her away.

"I just want to be *me* for a time. Not your wife, not my momma's daughter, not even Christian's mom. I need to do some things I want to do."

"You can do anything you want," Jerome almost yelled.

"I can do anything I want. But unfortunately, I need to leave to do it!" With a smack of my lips, I got up and began to walk away.

The first thing I had to do was find someone to watch five-year-old Christian. Fortunately, my cousin Leslie volunteered. She is an angel. She told me to go find myself and not return until I was victorious.

"Come back with a smile or don't come back," she said. "And don't worry about Chris. He'll be fine."

With a tear in my eye and a fear of the unknown, I began to walk away.

The next (and last) person on my list was my momma. I began to hum a song I had heard at church. I didn't know the words but I just hummed something. Made my own song. You know we gotta do that sometimes.

I walked up to Momma's brownstone, took a deep breath, and tapped on the door. The smell of fresh-baked sweet potato pie greeted me. I'd be leaving that behind too.

My mother is a real 'country cooker.' You won't find a box mix in the house. Everything is made from scratch. She is always cooking for some dinner at the church.

"Momma," I began when she let me into the kitchen. "I'm headin' out early next week."

"Y'all going on another family vacation?" she asked as she made another pie crust.

"No, Momma. I'm leavin' Jerome."

She stopped what she was doing and looked up at me. "What he do to you?"

"Nothing, Momma. Haven't you ever wanted to be more than Daddy's wife, or me and Julianne's mother?"

I followed her to the sink. She told the air that she sure raised one crazy child.

"I don't want no part of this, girl." She looked angry. "If you is leavin' for some liberated-woman dreams, you can count me out for support. You got more money than I ever had in all my life, and you want me to help you leave it?"

"I'm sorry if you don't understand, Momma, but I've just got to go."

"Then go! But don't expect us to be here waitin' with open arms when you come back."

I grabbed my purse and a paper towel to wipe my tears and walked out the door.

I knew she wouldn't understand. She was hurt. The big dreams she had for me and Julianne weren't coming together. Julianne was already divorced and it looked like I probably would be too.

I left my momma's house and didn't look back. I picked up the keys (from the devil himself) and walked away.

I Must Crawl Before I Can Walk

Jerome didn't come home for the next two days.

Probably doesn't want to face the fact that I'm serious about leavin', I thought as I packed a few things in my duffel bag—one of the few things I had bought myself. I threw in two pairs of jeans, four of my favorite shirts, a pair of high-tops, and two pair of socks (one black and one white).

In the zipper section, I put a bag of crackers, $28.00 in bills, and $3.25 in change (for bus fare).

Tired of waiting for Jerome, I left without saying good-bye.

My friend Anita works for Greyhound and she got me a charity ticket. I had to pick a destination. I chose a town in Kansas. Don't know anyone there, and the trip will take about three days. She gave me eight tokens to use for food.

I looked at the tokens in my hand and sighed. *This is what you wanted, right?* I asked myself.

While my ticket was being printed, Anita told me I have guts. "Lots of women probably want to do what you're doing but they can't see themselves leaving unhappy houses, empty marriages, and selfish children for something better."

But I had a good marriage and a wonderful son. And yet, I was still walking.

Am I normal?

The bus ride wasn't too bad. I sat in the middle part of the bus, near the window. I only had to change buses once. We traveled late at night so no one saw my tears.

There were all types of people on the bus, going different directions for various reasons.

I wondered about one woman with two young children. Was she like me?

But she has her children. I left my child behind!

Okay, Janelle, this is no time for a pity party, my conscience told me. So I opened my notebook and drew out a plan for what I'd do upon my arrival to my new city.

1. Locate a YWCA. I needed a place to live.
2. Find a job. This was a must.
3. Don't look back. Just look ahead.

At the first bus station, I had thirty minutes before my next bus arrived. In the ladies' restroom I was greeted by overflowing toilets and filthy trash cans. I pulled a paper towel out of the container and washed my face in the dirty sink.

So far I had only used three of my tokens. And I had half a box of crackers left. I stuck one in my mouth and joined the line that was forming to get on the next bus.

A white man spoke to me as I was getting on the bus. "Where you headin'?" he asked.

I told him the name of the town.

"That's a nice part of Kansas. You got family or friends there?"

"No," I told him, beginning to get annoyed. "No friends either. I'm just going somewhere to start my life over."

"Well, good luck," he said. "Not too many Fortune 500 companies there. Most of the women work as waitresses or in one of the four factories they got there."

I'd never done either in my life.

I thanked him for the information, though. He was just trying to make conversation. I knew I shouldn't be so hard on anybody who tried to talk to me.

When I began to get off the bus at my destination, he pushed something into my hand. "Be careful," he said as he walked away.

In my hand I found $2.00 in change. I now had thirty dollars to my name. Things were looking better.

Taking My First Steps

Athens, Kansas. My new home.

I needed to start getting myself together. I had two crackers left, about thirty dollars, and I needed a place to stay.

While walking across the street, I saw a YWCA. On the outside was a bent hanging sign that read, "Rooms for Rent."

No time to be scared, Janelle. After whispering a quick prayer I walked into the messy office.

A nice-looking lady behind the counter introduced herself as Tavina. She and her husband ran the place, she informed me.

"Rooms run $11.50 for three days," she said. "If you want one, you can have it, but you can only stay for up to thirty-five days."

I gave her the money and got a receipt.

"This is Tuesday; that's when we offer the roomers pork chops with rice and gravy and a vegetable for three dollars. Soft drink is included."

My wallet was getting slim, but I had to eat. I gave her another $3.00.

Tomorrow, I'd go job hunting. Where, I didn't know. But with money running out it didn't really matter.

The food was cold but good. The other roomers seemed okay. One woman, Elayne, sat next to me. "Me and my children are moving out on Friday," she told me between bites. "Who did you come here to see?"

"No one," I said. "I'm just starting my life over."

Why am I telling her this? I don't even know her. But she made me feel comfortable.

"Mrs. Tavina's niece needs some help at the restaurant," Elayne said.

"Thank you, Lord," I said. "And thank you, too, Elayne."

After dinner I went downstairs and asked Mrs. Tavina about the job.

"Bobby Joe's Diner does need a waitress. Have you ever waited tables?" She looked at my clothes, sizing me up.

"No. But I do need a job."

"Be at Bobby Joe's at eleven a.m. sharp. If you can handle the lunch crowd, the job is yours. If you're good, your tips will show it."

Shock came upstairs to my room with me. I had a job. My first job ever! I was on my way.

Today I Crawled a Bit

I'd never worked so hard in my life. Pouring drinks, making small talk, getting food. But Tavina was right. The tips showed I was doing something right.

After my first six-hour day, I had $53.00 in tips. I paid for a few more days on my room. Bought a loaf of bread and some peanut butter.

Tomorrow, I may splurge and buy a paper.

When I woke the next morning at six, the sun was shining a bit too brightly. I showered and changed clothes.

I arrived at work by 10:50.

"You gonna do real good," Miles the cook told me.

My second day's tips added up to a measly $12.00. But that was okay. I was learning things about myself.

For one thing, I realized that I liked to draw. I always had a pencil in my hand. I also made some mean barbeque sauce.

Sunday after work I had an appointment to look at a new apartment.

I'm Just About There

I have been gone from my family for six months. I left the YWCA a long time ago. Mrs. Tavina and Bobby Joe come see me most days.

I work part time at the Afro-Centrically Art Museum across from the diner. Taking a few classes at Northern Heights College is the next step for me.

I called Jerome, but he hung up on me.

The divorce papers have been served, and I may get to see my son for three days in July.

I did the right thing. I know I did. I have a peace about myself, of who I am and where I want to go. Sadly, I had to leave my family behind to get there.

In the End, Walking Upright

Two years ago, I was a divorced woman in a one-bedroom apartment with no furniture. I now own my condo, have a used car, and own—yes, own—Afro-Centrically Art Museum.

Thank you for letting me share a piece of my life with you. Here's what I would like to leave you with. If you want to do something, be something, or go somewhere, just do it. Don't wait twenty years for a dream. And don't let your dream become a nightmare.

Janelle Miller
CEO and Founder of Tiara Art

What's Your Name?

Karen, Linda, Elayne;
Those are too-common names.

Jane, Alice, Sally;
Yuck! Too plain.

Karla, Esther, Grace;
Way old.

Tracy, Melissa, Michelle;
Sound like homecoming queens.

Kadeisha, Tamara, Melonné;
All three wrapped in one.

Makeisha, Shakeisha, Laneisha;
Just call me Eisha.

Simone or Sahara;
Was my mom in the desert when she gave
birth?

Talisha, Arienna;
Gotta be different.
Be my own person.

Just a simple name for this girl
Nothing to hard, nothing to plain
Love it or leave it
It's all in the name

Wish I Were a Fly on the Wall

You know the saying, "Wish you were here"? Well, guess what? I am there!

I am the fly on the wall at the church. Not your church, not your mama's church, just "the church."

My boy, Leroy, told me how to get in one Friday. They had a fish fry and left the kitchen door open and I went right on in.

I stayed a couple of weeks. Had me a good ol' time in the house of the Lord.

As a fly on the wall, I have preferred seating. Any pew I want is mine. No assigned seats for us flies!

Join me for a walk down memory lane.

Skeletons in the Closet

I stayed in the kitchen for a few minutes. The crumbs from freshly fried trout, catfish nuggets, and perch were good. When I was full, I decided to check out the rest of the building.

Down the hall from the choir room I found a closet. Way, way back I discovered some old bones. Those bones had a story to tell.

Seems about thirty-five years ago, beloved Pastor Tommie was in a drug rehab clinic. He wasn't there to minister to the people, but as a client! His habit back then was costing $85 a day (in saints' money).

No one knew, except maybe Trustee Vern, but that man is loyal. He just gave the pastor the money.

Loyal Vern went to his grave mighty early. Death certificate said "natural causes." He took the secret with him. But those bones in the back of the closet know all about it.

As long as the church clean-up crew keeps doing a shabby job, those bones are gonna stay back there in the corner.

Pastor Tommie doesn't go to rehab any more. But he does see Dr. Martin for an "asthmatic cough." But the phones know that cough is a result of not getting his "medicine."

Well, I'm a fly, so I gotta fly. Have to check out the rest of this church. But thanks for the info, guys. I'll try to catch you on my way out.

The Anointed Voices

Usually, when colored folks join a church, they check out the choir right away. If it's decent, they might consider joining that church. If not, they will remain visitors. 'Cause it's the choir that can "sing you happy" or put you to sleep.

Now, this church I'm in right now, they got it going on! Burgundy and cream-colored robes with the initials A.V. in the left corner. New members have to attend six rehearsals before they're allowed to sing with this group.

Well, since it's Tuesday, might as well stay for their choir rehearsal.

Now, I just know that when the choir director, Pam, read the announcements last Sunday she said rehearsal would start at 7:30 sharp. She even put an emphasis on the word *sharp*.

She was loud enough to wake the sleeping deacons. But it looks like the folks from the choir didn't hear her.

The clock on the wall says 7:45, but there are only five out of forty-five active members here. Where are all the singers and musicians?

Sister "Forever Faithful" Tiffany was here at 7:20. No matter what "issues" are going on in her life, Tiffany is always at the church whenever the doors are open. And this girl has to ride the bus, with two transfers, and then walk the last block to church. So how come those other members, some with two or three cars, aren't here?

The Section-8 apartment she shares with her grandmother, two brothers (who float in and out), and two sisters (who have four children between them) is very well kept.

And God uses Tiffany's second-soprano voice. That girl has a real anointing on her!

As soon as a saved young man of God starts believing God for a wife, I think the Lord will direct him toward Tiff.

Well, I see Maxie, the choir president, has arrived. And it's only 7:51. She was at Flo's Beauty Shop and Spa. Why that girl makes her hair appointments at 6:00 on choir rehearsal day is beyond me.

Oh, look! Her hair is only two colors this week. And there seems to be a bit of weave up there. I like the green and gold stripes. Must mean she's planning to wear a green suit with gold shoes this Sunday.

She clears her throat. "Rehearsal will now begin, people," she says.

No apologies for being late, I see. Just business as usual.

"You know the formation," she says, not quite stifling a yawn.

First and second sopranos take the first two rows. Altos and high tenors sit behind them, and deep voices are in the back.

The musicians still aren't in the sanctuary. They aren't anywhere on the church premises. They're all at T.J.'s house watching the hip-hop awards on pay-per-view!

T.J. is the head organist. The rest of the band follows his lead. Wherever T.J. is, that's where they'll be. Apparently they don't have minds of their own.

Maxie starts off the rehearsal by listing the songs they will sing on Sunday. Then she says, "Now, people, we need to meet downstairs after Sunday school is dismissed for prayer. Pastor Tommie has some concerns because some of you are not attending Sunday school. Now, I am guilty myself. But it's all I can do to get here in time to put on my robe."

Whatever!

Brother Joe "Wandering Eye" Simmons jumps in. "But Pastor said we are all to be here for Sunday school."

Now, he can't talk about people not being in their proper places when he's so busy looking at Sister Elise and Sister Tayla…but not Sister Kevra, his wife of eighteen years!

What you see on Sunday is definitely not what happens on Tuesday. Seems the Anointed Voices needs a special refreshing to come their way.

"You got a problem?" Maxie glares at Joe.

You can practically feel the ice in the sanctuary.

Oh, the saints of the Most High God are having some attitudes tonight, I see!

The musicians make their appearance at 8:30.

"T.J.," bellows Maxie, "where have you been?"

"Stuck in traffic," T.J. says.

"Yeah," the others say.

This choir needs some dedicated members. Yeah, I know, they won the Congressional Choir of the Year award three years straight. But these folks got serious things going on.

Well, the choir went over all their songs till everything sounded just right to Maxie. They dismissed at ten. There's no way they should be leaving already. But they have a few bars to go to…and that's not musically speaking!

As everyone moseys out, I overhear a few of the members talking in hushed tones. Seems choir elections are next June. Tazare has already announced that she plans on taking the top spot from Maxie.

Thank goodness I can fly outta here! I need to take a breather.

Leroy, my main boy, is at another church. Seems they are having a church dinner in two weeks, and the food is there for the taking.

If you're looking for a church home, this place doesn't seem to be so bad.

Next Friday is the annual business meeting. This is the time for resignations, firings (oh, yeah, folks get fired from church positions!), and so forth.

It's gonna be a hot Friday night this year. Maybe I'll invite Frank to join me there so I don't have to take all this in by myself. He's a good fly-friend. I hope he can get up from the East Side.

Chicken Dinners (and Fish Too!)

The usher board, under the direction of the head usher, Brother Foster, is having a fundraiser. They want to leave the "White Blouse/Black Skirt" syndrome and go with white blouses and purple skirts. Realizing that this venture will take money, they decided to have a chicken dinner.

Lots of problems can be solved with food. Maybe that's why half of the folks here are, shall we say, kinda plump!

Sister Edda will fry the chicken. Everyone will get either a breast and a wing or a drumstick and thigh. No gizzards, livers, or backs. Charmaine will go over to her house Saturday night and help cut up the birds.

Mabel makes the best macaroni and cheese this side of Jackson, Mississippi. But you do have to pay her $3.50 per pan. She is a "retired" usher (actually, a sat-down usher) who still helps out when needed.

Selma and Charles (husband and wife) will do the greens, yams, and okra. I heard Selma say she was going to First for Foods to get her greens 'cause their turnips were the best. Probably sixteen bunches will do it.

Now, the yams will come from Fred's Market. Charles will get those on Friday.

Casinetta will make the rolls. When her husband passed last June, she got a job at the bread store on 39th Street. That woman knows how to make rolls that melt in your mouth. She brushes sweet honey butter over those things like there is no tomorrow.

Of course, nobody wanted to donate anything. Everybody asked the secretary for money to buy the ingredients they need.

The ushers are having a meeting at Brother Foster's house to finalize everything. His wife, Diane, is not saved and she is not happy about these people coming to her home. She is cordial, though. Their house is next door to the church, so I fly over there easily.

"I think we should sell the dinners for ten dollars," Carmen says. "These folks got money and it will be First Sunday."

"Ten dollars might be tough," remarks George. "Especially to the folks who gave to the building fund."

According to Lorene, the church journalist-at-large, not everyone is giving. She should know. Her nose is up in everything.

They settle on $7.50. Sweet iced tea and lemonade will be free.

Mother Tompkins can't cook, but she says she will sell sweet potato pies after the dinner and give the ushers a small portion.

Well, the dinner day is here. The whole church smells like food. Deacon Fletch is frying some perch but he only has a few fillets.

"Yes, you can write a check," says Traci, who filled in for Pam to do the announcements. "No, it can't be postdated."

I'm having a ball! The greens got a bit of onion on the top; the macaroni and cheese is sizzling hot.

I thought Frank was coming this way. Wonder what's keeping him so long?

All in all the dinner was a success. The ushers raised $520. The Capris and the Turners still owe on their dinners, but Brother Foster is a nice man.

Frank made it up. After the dinner we sat in the back chillin'. We were stuffed to the max. The trash men don't come till Thursday, so we're set for a few days!

I hear Pastor Tommie wants a meeting with the executive board before the business meeting. He usually leaves his window cracked in his office, so Frank and I won't have any problem getting in.

Pastor Calls a Meeting

Pastor Tommie asked the church receptionist, Carla, to get on the phone and call all the auxiliary heads to schedule a meeting on Thursday at 7:00. The church attorney, Brian Grims, will be in attendance. My, my, my, what a time this will be. Unfortunately for me and Frank, though, there will be no food served at this meeting.

The first phone call went out to Sister Yvette Riggens, the Sunday school director. After six rings the phone picked up.

"Sister Riggens, this is Carla from church."

"I saw the number on my caller ID," she said in an irritated tone. "I thought I made it clear that I do not want calls at my home before eleven a.m."

"I'm calling on behalf of the pastor," Carla replied in a nice, humble tone.

"Oh? And what does the pastor need?" Sister Riggens asked in a flat voice.

"There is a meeting this Thursday at 7:00 p.m. You are asked to be there"

"And if I'm not?"

"Can't say, ma'am. I'm just doing as asked."

"Well, you can tell the pastor that I have been informed. I will be there. And I would like a few minutes to speak."

"So noted," said Carla. Then she quickly hung up the phone.

Carla did not like to talk with Sister Riggens. She was mean to everyone, which could explain why teachers sometimes didn't show up for their classes and why enrollment has dropped from 175 to 68. The young people never knew who would be their teacher from Sunday to Sunday.

Carla called seven "auxies," but only reached four: T.J. Parker, the Minister of Music; Sunday School Director Yvette Riggens; Youth Leader Gregory Moore; and the Ministerial Alliance Chair, Michael Lamonte.

She had to leave messages for the others. I think she was glad she wouldn't have to attend this meeting.

Time for a Break

Frank found out that the delivery truck would be up the street at Connie's Shop-N-Go till six p.m. Since the store is only a block up the way, we had time stop by there, see what was being thrown out, get a bite to eat, and still make it back to the church in time for the meeting.

Today the only food going out was some old bread and lunchmeat. But it was enough.

While we were there, we saw two other fly-friends, Harry and Sal. They've been hanging out at Claire's French Café. We caught up on old times for a while and then split.

A Not-So-Nice Meeting of the Minds

When Frank and I flew through the crack in the church office, we heard Pastor calling on the name of the Lord.

"Lord, I need a word from You. This is Your temple; it's for Your glory. Lord, I need to know that You are with me."

He gets up, wipes a few drops of sweat off his forehead, and waits for the members to arrive.

Everyone is finally present and accounted for. The pastor asks Elder Abner to say the prayer. After casting out all things that are not like God and blessing the members, the meeting begins.

"First of all," Pastor says quietly, "I want you all to realize that I do nothing without consulting the almighty Father."

Somebody said, "Amen."

"I have decided to make some changes in our church structure, effective tonight." Without blinking an eye, he said, "The first order of business is the Sunday school department. Sister Regina Wells will now be our director."

Sister Riggens raises her hand. "May I comment?"

"No comments or questions," replies the pastor, his voice rising. "I have been dissatisfied with numerous things in that department for quite some time. Enrollment, teacher effectiveness, offering. Need I say more?"

Man, if my boy Lloyd the mouse was here, you could hear him walking on through.

Sister Riggens asks another question. "Then may I be dismissed, since it appears that I don't need to be here?" Now *her* voice is rising!

"If you wish," Pastor says.

With a huff she gathers her things, wipes a tear, and slams the door.

"We will now discuss the music ministry," Pastor continues without missing a beat.

T.J. shifts in his chair, but holds his head up.

"Brother Parker, I have been informed by various choir members that there are some problems with the choir president and with you. You have thirty days to prove that you want to be a vital part of this congregation. In the meantime, your salary is on hold. On the eighteenth of next month your position will be reevaluated."

T.J. sweating big time!

"I will open the floor if any of you have questions," Pastor says.

No one mutters a word. I'm not sure they're even breathing.

"I am satisfied with the Youth Empowering Youth program and the Ministerial Alliance," Pastor says.

Sister Regina is cool, and she's the pastor's daughter-in-law, so she won't mess up.

Annual Church Business Meeting

The meeting is scheduled to start at 7:00. What's this? Saints are gathering at 6:20! I guess folks just wanna be in the know.

By 7:00 every pew is filled. People who show up in the nick of time end up sitting in the lobby. They need a sign that says "Standing Room Only."

I can feel the tension and excitement in the air. Folks who didn't even come to First Sunday are here.

I guess the news has spread about Sister Riggens being fired. Lots of the members didn't like her anyway. They didn't know Regina would be taking over, but it will be welcomed news.

T.J. is sitting in the first row. That alone could give a few of the church mothers a heart attack!

Tyrone, Leon, and Kincaid are right behind him in the second row. Guess the talk T.J. had with Tyrone got through to him. Tyrone probably put a bug in the other band members' ears.

No check till the eighteenth is going to put a dent in his spending for sure. As assistant manager of supplies at Denco, a computer company, finances can get tight. When sales have been low, the money from the church has come in mighty handy.

Brother Hosea opened the meeting with prayer. He cast out demonic forces, called on hellfire and brimstone, then the people said, "Amen." I even said it. Frank too! Man, he had us shaking!

Sister Claudette sang a moving rendition of "The Blood that Jesus Shed for Me." As she hit the high notes at the end, Pastor Tommie walked in.

First Lady Venisha opened up the business meeting by playing a song. No one knew the words, but she kept tinkering away on the keyboard. Pastor Tommie was tapping his feet, even though she was playing a slow song.

Pastor Tommie started off with a few general announcements. Then he prayed, but not like Brother Hosea.

"As you know," Pastor started off, "this is the time when changes come to our assembly. Change is good, saints. We are moving up, not back." He held his breath for a moment. "After careful consideration and much prayer, I have made some changes. I will list four of them and then open the floor for a few minutes of discussion."

"Here are the changes I have made." He looked at his notes. "Number one, the Sunday school department will now be in the capable hands of Sister Regina Wells. She will need two new teachers."

She needs two new teachers because the two who have been teaching have moved their membership to Pastor Seinz's church.

Sister Riggens's name was not mentioned. I looked around, but she wasn't even there.

"Number two, the music ministry. The teen choir will purchase new robes. The senior choir will sing for the Easter sunrise service. And we need to purchase a new drum set."

Man, is it quiet in this place tonight!

"The choir will have elections in two weeks. I will need the names of those intending to run for office."

"I can provide that, sir," TJ said.

Sir? I've never heard T.J. give that much respect to anyone! The saints must be wondering what's going on!

Tazare will run for choir president against Maxie, who is at Flo's again. This is one meeting she should not have been late to.

One thing I've noticed about Tazare is her love for the household of faith. She is not into titles. She just wants to see things done right. "Do everything as unto the Lord" is her motto.

She tried to give Maxie some suggestions, but they all just hit the wall. She believed God would work things out in His own timing. Now it's time for her to move up in her anointing.

"Number three, the ministerial alliance."

"The ministers' retreat has to be postponed," Elder Lamonte interrupted. "Minister Dawkins resigned as head of the baptismal committee due to health reasons. Sister Edna will be at the King's Highway Revival next Wednesday through Friday."

"I didn't receive notification of this," Pastor Tommie said.

"Sister Edna said she had cleared it with you," Elder Lamonte said.

"Well, she didn't."

Seems that revival will not be happening.

Elder Lamonte moved on. "All Ministerial Alliance dues have been collected and sent to the District Secretary, Sister Charlene Towers, in Memphis."

Man! It's already 9:00 and this meeting is still going on. I saw Maxie show up around 8:30. I noticed orange stripes in her hair, so I guess everybody knows what color she'll be wearing on Sunday.

Brother Foster came in after her. He works late at Stone's Hardware, so he has a good excuse for his tardiness.

Sister Riggens called the lobby phone around 8:45 to say she had the flu. Tamisha didn't bother to tell anyone she called.

"Number 4," Pastor said. "Youth Empowering Youth."

Brother Gregory Moore reported that they were staying within their budget. They had raised $289 on their last candy sale. "All youth wanting to go on the next outing need to sign up no later than Sunday night."

He also has tickets to the Gospel Expo concert, if anyone wants them.

Pastor Tommie said he was very pleased with the work his nephew, Greg, was doing with the young people. Greg used to date Maxie, but that soon grew cold. He was considering asking Tazare if she wanted to go to dinner with him.

The young people were going door to door witnessing on Saturday. Pastor said he hoped everything went well.

There were some issues going on. Two teens were with child, and Brother Gregory was encouraging them to get their lives straight. Brother Jackson had asked the young people to write his son, Kendrick, at the county jail. That plan would soon unfold.

Brother Henry has a video from the marriage seminar. Seems strange to me that he would go to a seminar when he is seventy years old and a widower. His wife just passed a month ago. Is he already out looking?

Applications for the Howard Grayson Memorial Scholarship are in the lobby. The deadline to apply is in three weeks. The church has four graduating seniors who could all use the money to further their education.

The Sleek Steppers will be at NorthTowne Mall on Saturday. The saints don't seem to mind encouraging the steppers; it's their director, Taish "Got an Attitude" Jones, they don't have time for.

Sister Serena pleaded that something be done about the flies in the church office. Pastor agreed to look into calling an exterminator.

This is certainly not the news I came to the church for!

The meeting was dismissed at 10:00. Some of the young people went to Foley's Steak and Cheese House for a bite. The older folks went home.

Guess I need to be hunting for a new home too. Sister Serena mentioned "flies." Here I thought I was the only one.

I decide to go to the back of the church to chill out. Somebody threw a bologna sandwich back there that missed the trash can altogether.

Frank decides to take off. He is going over to China One Café. He promised to see if they have room for me there, in case I have to leave the church.

But I don't plan on deserting the place right away. One little teeny-weeny complaint and they want to call the exterminator? Makes me almost mad enough to blow this joint! But if I do, well, to coin a phrase from my favorite movie, *The Ex-Terminator*: "I'll be back!"

Choir Takes a Vote

Well, it's voting day for the choir. All forty-five members (including those on leave of absence and the sat-down members) came out.

The elections started before rehearsal so the new president could start his or her first practice with some comments. Elections were to begin at 6:00 sharp.

Maxie arrived at 5:34. Her hair was in a simple French roll, with no added colors. She is wearing a casual peach skirt-and-jacket set with low black pumps. Talk about a 180-degree turnaround!

T.J. arrived at 5:45. He received approval from the pastor on all names submitted, with one minor change. Pastor Tommie didn't think the choir needed a sergeant-at-arms.

Of course, Pastor never made it to rehearsals so he had no idea how out of hand these folks can get.

T.J. has one week left of his thirty-day watch, and it looks like he's going to come out on the good side. Of course, the talks he had with Tyrone and the band sure helped.

The elections were called to order by Maxie. "As you're all aware" she said, "the Anointed Voices changes leadership every two years. Only members in good standing are eligible to vote."

She shot a look at Kandrea. Everyone in the church knows Kandrea is with child. They also know it is not an immaculate conception.

Does anyone see the girl is trying to get her life straight? She may not need constant reminders of her upcoming due date. The belly that moves tirelessly is enough of a reminder. And the baby's father has skipped town.

"I will now read the names on the ballot," Maxie announced.

Pencils were provided with each ballot. First Lady Venisha and Trustee Robertson were assigned to count votes and let the choir members know the results by 6:45.

The list of names were provided in this order:

President
Maxie Clark
Tazare Stevens

Vice President
Kelly Turner (unopposed)

Church Secretary
Diane Silencia
Toby Rightman

Neither Diane nor Toby have any clerical skills. Since Maxie knew she was going to win, she could care less which one of these two won.

What she didn't know is that Tazare had been teaching Diane to type. Even though she was hard of hearing, the girl was a quick learner.

Now, Toby could type, but she was nonchalant about the choir. She came to rehearsal if and when she felt like it. If she knew the songs they were singing and she liked them, she was there. If not, she wasn't and she didn't bother to call.

Maxie should have gotten to know her members just a little bit more.

Assistant Secretary
No names

Whoever lost the secretary position would become the assistant.

Treasurer
John Palmer
Kate Winsley

John has been the choir treasurer for six years. He's good with figures, and since they never have more than $129 in their account, he never has to work hard.

Now, if the choir ever did raise money, he might be in trouble. He had a habit of visiting Cortino's Casino when he was down and out. The less money he had to deal with at the church, the better off he was.

Another choir member Maxie didn't know about.

Tazare, if elected, had no plans to include John. Her plans included Kate Winsley. She's the new kid on the block. A babe in Christ. Quiet and reserved, Kate knows how to handle money.

Her husband, Todd, has been out of work for seven months. With Kate staying at home with the three children, money has been tighter than tight.

Todd's severance pay ran out three weeks ago, but God has provided. The rent is caught up, utilities are still on, and, even their tithes are up to date!

Pantry is full every week too. The woman knows how to stretch a dollar and still have change leftover. Many in the church don't know of her situation, but she will be a vital asset to this change in leadership. And believe me, changes are coming.

First Lady Venisha enters the sanctuary around 6:48. Everyone has been waiting for her arrival with anticipation of new things to follow.

"Well, folks," she says as she breezes in, "all praises be to God!"

"All praises be to God," the choir members echo.

"I will now read the results of the Anointed Voices general elections," she says. "After that, I will ask all those elected to come up front, and the new president to give remarks." She smiles. "Congratulations and may God be with you all."

Her first announcement: "For President...Tazare Stevens!"

The applause was so loud I'm surprised it didn't set off the alarm. (Everyone clapped but Maxie.)

Taz raised her hand and quietly said, "Thank You, Jesus."

"Vice President...Kelly Turner. Secretary...Diane Silencia. Assistant Secretary...Toby Rightman. Treasurer...Kate Winsley."

Kate screamed, mostly in shock.

John was just as shocked, but he didn't scream. Gasped, though. He will become Assistant Treasurer. That will give him more time to gamble without the guilt.

"We will now have remarks from our new president," T.J. said.

As Taz stood, I could feel a change in the sanctuary.

"All good things come from God," she started off. After thanking everyone for their votes of confidence, she let the members know their work has just begun. "This is not a social club, but a vital ministry. We are to help the hurting, the lost, and the happy folks."

She won't be making major changes, but at least she has the backing of the saints

Frank came by to tell me that China One Café is not all that great. Seems the health department closed them down last year because of flies.

So he's been hanging out at Shorelake Nursing Home. The kitchen staff wastes food daily. One man's garbage is our next meal!

I told him as soon as I have to leave the church, I'll catch him over there.

To the Pastor's House

Pastor Tommie is on his way home. I see a window left open in the black Toyota Camry. I fly in to check out his "spread." I make myself at home in the backseat while he picks up the last of the papers he was going through.

I hang out on the roof while he drives. Zipping down the highway at sixty-five, with about two hundred eyes, it's a pretty cool view!

First Lady Venisha has called twice, saying dinner is ready. He is not rushing home for her cooking, but leaving the church will help his headache.

Pastor Tommie took over Stonewater Temple after Reverend Tyler passed away. Sometimes he thinks the saints got to the Rev and caused that massive stroke. The man was too young to die, only fifty-nine. But church folks can kill you if you let 'em.

Mother Tyler still receives a nice allowance from the church. She's on the phone to him by ten a.m. if her check isn't in the mail on the third of each month.

Many times his old habits have tried to call him back. Pastor has given his life fully to the Lord, though. The only time he plans to see Duvall's rehab center again is if (God forbid) one of the saints has to go there. It does happen, you know.

There are still skeletons in his (and Venisha's) closet, but he plans to keep them there. He still can't believe how God could take a dope-addicted guy like him and call him to the ministry, but He did!

Venisha has the table set and dinner ready when he walks in. She gives him a quick kiss and tells him to go wash his hands.

The Duke Ellington CD playing in the background is soothing, but not gospel. He takes it out and puts in "The Mighty Clouds of Joy."

After a fine dinner of chicken and dumplings, the pastor decides to retire in his office.

Looking over his calendar, he thinks back on the past few months. They've been rough, but God has blessed. He is elated over the new choir administration. He prayed that God would remove selfish and self-righteous Maxie Clark.

The Ministerial Alliance is coming together just fine. He may consider going on vacation and leaving Elder Lamonte in charge.

The ushers have raised the money for their much-needed uniforms.

He goes to check the answering machine. Venisha rarely answers the phone. She usually doesn't feel like being bothered with the saints.

Sixteen messages! My goodness. Can't anyone get on their own knees and pray?

Some of the messages are immediately deleted (telemarketers). Sister Serena called twice about the "fly issue." (I'm starting not to like her.)

Mother Catskill needs a ride to the prayer meeting. (She refuses to ride the church van.) The heat is fixed in the fellowship hall.

After some small talk with Venisha and a few moments of playtime with Josiah, it's off to bed.

Tomorrow is another day.

Guess I'm stuck here. I'll make my bed in the kitchen, since some food was left out.

Pastor Tommie is leaving early in the morning for the church and I want to go back there. Got dizzy tonight with the roof ride, though. I'll have to ride in the backseat tomorrow.

The Deacons Take a Stand

Deacon Lester can't believe it. For the fourth time in six months, the Bennington family needs a loan. They have yet to pay off the last one ($529) for their rent.

As head of the Benevolence Committee, he sees applications all the time. The same group of saints are always in need. If the church didn't have this to offer, I'm sure the folks would make it somehow.

Countless times, he has asked Pastor Tommie to remind the saints that the church is not a bank. But, Pastor is a man of compassion and he will just keep helping and bailing people out.

If it were up to Deacon Les, he'd make the saints responsible for their own lives.

The Sumners have applied for $210 to get their clunker repaired. They had fallen on hard times and Sister Rhonda is using the car to get back and forth to work.

Howell, on the other hand, is sitting at home with a worker's compensation injury. Dr. Pester said he could have been back at work with light duty. But he never took the note to the personnel office.

Chantelle needs $75.80 for schoolbooks. That will be approved with no problem. When she was an honor student in college, the church helped her all the way through her studies.

Deacon Lester was going to have a sit-down talk with Pastor Tommie about the growing needs of the saints. The church will have to put off getting the new roof as long as the saints have "needs." There are other things the church requires, but money is going out the door faster than it can come in.

"Pastor," Lester said one day when the two men met for lunch at the Chip and Dip Deli, "we have to take a stand when it comes to lending the saints money."

"What's the problem?" Pastor Tommie took a bite of his tuna melt.

"The problem is, we are helping the same saints all the time, sometimes every month."

"I'll make an announcement Sunday," he said, "that starting immediately, all requests for financial aid must be approved by me personally."

Pastor kept his word. After the general announcements, he rose to make a special announcement. From now on, he said, all saints requiring financial assistance must make a formal request two weeks in advance. "And there will be only one loan per six-month period," he added. "Oh, and the roof repairs will start Tuesday afternoon. So saints, please park your cars on the street till Saturday evening."

Pastor then announced that Celina Morten had received the scholarship. She will attend Jackson Community College starting in the fall. Her award amount was $1800.

"The exterminator will be here Friday," the pastor said.

I nearly gagged on the peanut butter crackers I'd been munching on.

"The building will be off limits while the man does his work. The flies should all be gone by Sunday."

Oh, I'll be gone before that!

Well, I guess all good things must come to an end sometime. Guess I'll check out the Shorelake Nursing Home. But I have time for one more fly-through before I head out.

Saying Good-bye

I took one last look at Stonewater Temple Church. Too bad I have to leave. I kinda like this place.

If that Sister Serena hadn't made such a fuss, I probably could have hung out a little while longer.

Pastor Tommie Downey and his wife, Venisha, have a job on their hands. The number of saints who are available to help and be a blessing to others sure is small.

126

I decided to check in on the Sunday service the day after the pest control people came by. I don't like having to watch everything from this outside window, but at least it's a cool morning.

Sister Elise read Matthew 9:37—the King James version, of course. "The harvest truly is plenteous, but the labourers are few." She got that right.

The ushers look really nice in their starched white blouses and purple skirts. They even have name tags now. Brother Foster is "cheezing"[4] all day and he deserves all smiles.

Anointed Voices, under the direction of Tazare Moore (her married name), came in singing so powerfully, I'm sure I felt the Holy Ghost hit the window. The presence of God is full in that place. Amen!

Tyrone and the band had it going on. A record producer named Mr. Breherst was in the sanctuary. After the service, he talked to Tyrone about making a CD. Tyrone told him to get together with T.J.

Looks like things have really come together with the music ministry.

I came back to visit several Sundays after that, always looking in from the outside window just in case.

Kandrea had a beautiful baby girl.

Sister Riggens moved to Akron, Ohio. Hopefully, she can get herself to doing God's work in a better way.

Maxie now sings with the Temple Praise Team. She has settled down and really turned over a new leaf.

Frank came with me last Sunday. I tried to go see the "skeletons in the closet" but couldn't even get in the door. Maybe next time.

We definitely plan to come back in the summer. Outdoor barbeques and fish fries will be calling our names. I noticed a new fly swatter in the kitchen, but I won't let that hinder me.

Like my favorite actor says, "I'll be back!"

Endnotes

[1] "Blessed Assurance," words by Fanny J. Crosby, 1873.
[2] Psalm 107:2, King James Version (KJV)
[3] Psalm 24:8, KJV
[4] To smile vibrantly

CREDITS

Cover photos and design concept:
William O'Kelley

How to Order a Book

- **Phone orders**
  - ❖ Toll-free order: **877-421-READ**

- **Online ordering**
  - ❖ www.Amazon.com
  - ❖ www.BarnesandNoble.com

- **At your local library or bookstore**
  - ❖ Ingram, Spring Arbor, and Appalachian Distributors

- **In your local area**

Washington
  - ❖ Oasis of Hope Center
    Greater Christ Temple Church
    1937 South G Street, Tacoma, WA 98405
    (253) 272-5679
    www.greaterchristtemple.org

Texas
  - ❖ Christ Temple Apostolic Church of El Paso

7959 Esther Rd	Mailing Address
El Paso, TX 79915	PO Box 13502
(915) 584-2072	El Paso, TX 79913

www.christ-temple.net

How to Contact Us

E-mail: william.okelley@us.army.mil

Thank You!

Printed in the United States
119519LV00002B/1/A

9 781414 104416